immersed in the waters of life

Rev. Joseph G. Diermeier

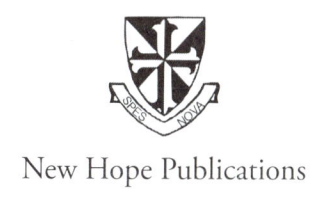

New Hope Publications

NIHIL OBSTAT:
Benedict T. Nguyen, M.T.S., J.C.L.
Censor Deputatus

IMPRIMATUR:
+Most Rev. Jerome E. Listecki, D.D., J.C.D.
September 15, 2009

For additional copies of this book, contact:
New Hope Publications
PO Box 10
New Hope, KY 40052
270-325-3061
www.newhope-ky.org

Ask for stock #3257.

Copyright 2009 by Rev. Joseph G. Diermeier
ISBN 978-1-892875-50-1

Cover photo: © Padal-Dreamstime.com

Contents

Introduction   v

1. **P**racticing Methods to Achieve Heart-to-Heart Conversation   1

2. **R**eviewing the Influence of the Covenant Between God and Humanity   9

3. **A**ccepting the Water From Jesus   19

4. **Y**earning for the Fire of the Holy Spirit   29

5. **E**xposing Myself to the One Who Knows Me Well   41

6. **R**esting in Love   51

Concluding Thought: Why Pray?   59

Introduction

Saint Therese of Lisieux, canonized in 1925 and named a Doctor of the Church in 1997, is remembered as one who prayerfully united her heart and soul with Christ and also allowed the grace of the Holy Spirit to help her reach out to others. In her autobiography, *Story of a Soul*, she describes how the "little way" had become her pathway to God.

For most of us, a variety of little ways usually becomes our route as well. Almost all spiritual growth occurs by means of little steps and in little ways. Prayer assists our growth and provides a reality check for faithfulness along the "little ways" of our own lives. The topic of prayer is the focus of these pages.

A word of explanation will help the reader to better understand the title of this short reflection. Imagine yourself next to a pool of water, wondering whether or not to get in. Someone from the pool calls, "Come on in, the water's fine!" Those are words of invitation. When we hear them we know that we are invited to enjoy a few moments of relaxation. Naturally, there may be some work involved, especially if we decide to swim and use strokes requiring muscle and strength. We might also simply rest, allowing the water to buoy our bodies. The important step is to get in – whether we jump, dangle our feet and gently lower ourselves in, dive, plunge, or whatever method we use, the necessary part of the invitation is to become *immersed.*

Prayer is about the human person in relationship with God. So is baptism, and therein lies the connection with water. Through the waters of baptism we are brought, actually incorporated, into the life of Jesus Christ and the love that Christ has for us. Baptism is about a relationship with Jesus; prayer is also about our relationship with Him. The outward sign of baptism is the pouring of water; with prayer, we allow the waters of baptism to pour over us as we lift our minds and hearts to God. In prayer we are united with Jesus, of whom Scripture says, "Rivers of living water will flow from within him" (Jn 7:38). Therefore, prayer and baptism are both about our relationship with

Christ in and through the Holy Spirit; prayer and baptism both involve being immersed in life-giving waters.

The invitation to prayer is like an invitation into the water. There are times when prayer requires muscle and strength, especially when the activities of our life which we bring to prayer are arduous. There are also times when prayer is like floating on our backs, simply relaxing in the presence of God. Whatever the situation, the water truly is great.

That doesn't mean that every situation will conclude "happily ever after." Rather, it means prayer somehow unites us to God both in joys and in struggles. The union with God is great, even when, and perhaps most especially when, our hearts ache. No matter how we come to prayer, the important thing is that we actually *get into the water*. Once in, whether we know it or not, the water possesses a greatness which mysteriously washes over us.

We are called to be professional in our prayer. Some people hear the word *professional* and associate it with an expert. Most of us do not claim to be experts in prayer. Nevertheless, by the very fact that we make the *Profession of Faith,* we are to be practitioners of prayer. Thus, prayer is part of our *professional* life – or at least should be. Some prayers are spontaneous, while others we know by rote. Some might be on the tips of our tongues and others tucked away in the recesses of our minds, only needing a little nudge to stir them loose. Prayer is an important key which unlocks the door to the mystery of Christ and our relationship with Him. Ultimately, prayer is good for the soul!

Every human being is both body and soul. The Latin word for soul is *anima* which is the root word for other words like *animation, alive,* and *exhilaration.* The soul is the animating part of our human person; without the soul we would not be alive. The soul is that which keeps us from falling apart. For example, when we die, the soul departs from the body. The body at that point starts to decompose, or at least the chemicals of which our body is made no longer work together. Without the soul, we fall apart. Any part of us that seems dead emotionally, psychologically, or spiritually is where we lack soul. Soul is the energy or the integration which keeps us animated and alive. Interestingly, when the body dies and the soul leaves the body, we usually refer to the body as a *corpse*. The Latin word *corpus* means "body." A corpse is no longer quite the full body it was when body and soul were united. A corpse is a *corpus* that is no longer complete, thus *corp_s*. The addition of the final letter "e" at the end of *corpse* reminds me of the word "empty," and how the dead body, no longer complete, has been emptied of soul. Prayer helps to nourish the soul by helping us to stay together emotionally and spiritually. An old saying is quite apt: "A life hemmed by prayer is less likely to unravel." The soul is what helps to keep our life hemmed.

There are great numbers of books as well as thousands of articles relating to various aspects of prayer. No one can fully exhaust the mystery and the riches to be found in prayer. The Catechism of the Catholic Church, teaching us by means of the four essential pillars of the Church's life, concludes by giving us in the fourth section a beautiful exposition of prayer. So why would I attempt to write something further? I certainly do not claim to have any new insights or new teachings. Nevertheless, because the topic is so expansive and because ongoing reflection about prayer and its influence in our lives can be helpful, I offer some ideas in six themes. The word *prayer* has six letters. Each letter will give insight into one of the themes. Thus, the six areas will include:

P — *P*racticing methods to achieve heart-to-heart conversation,
R — *R*eviewing the influence of the covenant between
      God and humanity,
A — *A*ccepting the water from Jesus,
Y — *Y*earning for the fire of the Holy Spirit,
E — *E*xposing myself to the One who knows me well, and
R — *R*esting in love.

Over the past few months I have occasionally been asked by parishioners to write more about prayer in the parish bulletin. Also, one day while I was out for a walk, a young man whom I did not recognize approached me and questioned, "Are you a priest?" I told him I was. With serious intent he proceeded to ask me for a few minutes of his time so that he could find ways to pray better. He told me that he had been distant from Christ and the Church but wanted to take some steps toward renewing this relationship. The gist of our conversation led to the discussion of the Lord's Prayer, the "Our Father."

The conversation with this fellow gave me the idea for my Lenten weekend Mass homilies; I would speak about the seven petitions of the "Our Father." As I prepared my thoughts surrounding the petition, "Thy Kingdom come," I realized I might be able to write something about prayer to further the message of the Kingdom. I write these thoughts, therefore, because the Holy Spirit might have been prompting the individuals who first approached me to write about prayer, or the young man who asked me how to pray, or my own desire to help "Thy Kingdom come." The words of Pope John Paul II add to the impetus behind this: "The Church needs to bring Jesus close to the people, making Him known to them and ensuring that the grace that flows from His pierced side as a source of living water reaches the hearts that thirst for the glory of the kingdom of heaven."[1]

I dedicate this reflection with gratitude to Monsignor John Francis Murphy, a dear friend and mentor who died on Oct. 4, 2005. I had the privilege of learning about priestly life and ministry from him during my year as a transitional deacon and in the subsequent years of our friendship until his death. His love for God, for the priesthood, for the People of God, and for prayer has guided my life.

I would also like to thank my bishop, Bishop Jerome Listecki, our diocesan chancellor, Ben Nguyen, and Capuchin Father Keith Clark for their encouragement with this project. Additionally, I am

---

[1] These words were spoken by Pope John Paul II in his *ad limina* address to the bishops of Brazil on February 7, 2003.

grateful to Archbishop Raymond Burke for his constructive guidance with some of the themes presented in this book.

May the prayer of Mary, from the first chapter of Luke's Gospel, remain on our lips as we reflect on the great waters that we enter when we pray. Her words are these: "My soul proclaims the greatness of the Lord; my spirit rejoices in God my Savior" (Lk 1:46-47).

Chapter 1

Practicing Methods to Achieve Heart-to-Heart Conversation

Scripture's insight:

The answer: Yes. The question: Was prayer important for Jesus? In the Gospel according to Matthew we read how Jesus, after feeding five thousand, "went up on the mountain by himself to pray. When it was evening he was there alone" (14:23). His time spent in prayer came, according to this Gospel tradition, right after He cured a number of people who were sick and after He fed five thousand disciples who had wanted to hear Jesus' preaching.

Can you imagine what might have been included in Jesus' prayer? Perhaps He gave thanks to His Father for having met those who were ill and who came to Him in faith. Perhaps He also gave thanks for the many who had come with open hearts to hear what He had to say about the Kingdom of God. Perhaps He was listening to the wind, realizing that His preaching was also being dispersed to the four corners of the globe by means of the disciples who had gathered earlier that day. Maybe Jesus was tired and was simply recollecting His thoughts and resting in the knowledge that it was the Father's will which He had accomplished once again. Maybe He smiled and asked His Father to bless the many children who had been dragged along by parents earlier in the day, especially the little children who might have had some illness or handicap, or even the spunky child who had been determined to let everyone around him know just how unhappy he was. Could Jesus have shed some tears, having been given the information that Herod had beheaded John, His cousin and the one from whom Jesus received baptism which marked the beginning of His public ministry? Might He have been seeking guidance from His Father for the next mission He would undertake? Whatever occurred in those moments, we realize that the time spent in prayer was a heart-to-heart conversation between Jesus and His Father.

We are told that after time spent in prayer, Jesus joined His disciples who were already out at sea and who were having a difficult time keeping the boat steady due to the high winds and waves. Jesus approached them, walking on water. If this was a first-time event, and by all indications it was, then it is understandable that the disciples would have been terrified. "At once Jesus spoke to them, 'Take courage, it is I; do not be afraid'" (14:27). Feelings of terror can play havoc on the heart; Jesus' words were intended to bring peace to their troubled hearts.

Then Peter, often described as a man of impetuous ways, said to Jesus, "Lord, if it is you, command me to come to you on the water" (14:28). Too late – he could not take the words back once they had been spoken. Jesus invited Peter to come, and without any initial hesitation, Peter attempted the walk. However, the winds were still strong and Peter became frightened. As he began sinking he cried out three words which can apply to every human relationship with Jesus: "Lord, save me." Those three words are a beautiful heart-to-heart conversation.

At the moment of Peter's cry for help, all eyes in the boat had to be upon the spectacular event occurring. This was a call of faith on Peter's part, and it was faith which the other disciples were also placing in Jesus to help their friend who had gotten himself quite literally into deep water. Peter's three words calling for help were his opportunity to practice heart-to-heart conversation with Christ.

Our own moments of heart-to-heart conversation with the Lord might be like Jesus' time with the Father before appearing to His disciples as He walked on the water. Our heart-to-heart encounters may contain sorrow, joy, a search for guidance, or simply feelings of gratitude. Our moments with the Lord might also be more like the encounter that Peter had with Jesus. We may be in troubled waters of our life and we might be calling out in faith for God's help, for Jesus' assistance. If so, a heart-to-heart conversation occurs. Actually, it is the encounter of our heart with the Divine Heart, the Sacred Heart, of Our Lord.

We can ask another question, and again the answer is *yes* if we take our own discipleship to Christ seriously: Is this kind of prayer, a heart-to-heart conversation with Jesus Christ, important in our lives?

The insight of companions who experience the waters:

Archbishop Fulton J. Sheen (1895-1979) placed his life at the disposal of Providence and through his radio and television appearances became almost a mainstay in many Catholic and non-Catholic households throughout the United States. His final book, an autobiography entitled *Treasure in Clay*, was published posthumously. He begins the work by writing: "Carlyle was wrong in saying that there is no life of a man faithfully recorded. Mine was! The ink used was blood, the parchment was skin, the pen was a spear."[2] Archbishop Sheen reminds the reader that the inside story to his own life is the cross of Jesus. He recounts his own failings as he reflects upon the crucifix: "In the crown of thorns, I see my pride, my grasping for toys in the pierced Hands, my flight from shepherding care in the pierced Feet, my wasted love in the wounded Heart." The archbishop's love for Christ prompted him to express his thought in this way: "My heart weeps at what ... the 'I' has done to the 'Thou,' what the professed friend has done to the Beloved."[3]

In these words we gain insight into Archbishop Sheen's personal relationship with Christ. These were words of deep love, written only after years of growth in an abiding relationship of love. When he speaks of the "I" and "Thou" or of the professed friend and the Beloved, Archbishop Sheen is demonstrating a beautiful heart-to-heart encounter with the Lord. He knows of the love of God for him and knows that his life would be radically altered were it not for the Divine Love permeating his life and all of creation.

The heart-to-heart encounter between the Lord and ourselves is well-expressed in a book written by Fr. Blaise Arminjon, S.J., entitled *The Cantata of Love: A Verse by Verse Reading of*

---

2 Fulton J. Sheen, *Treasure in Clay* (San Francisco: Ignatius Press, 1993) 7.
3 *Ibid.*

the Song of Songs.[4] Fr. Arminjon, who has assisted many in the development of the spiritual life, suggests the Song of Songs as a source whence we are able to discover God's abiding presence in our lives, a presence which translates as the Heart of God uniting with our own hearts. His insights also parallel what the Second Vatican Council offered to the Church in the Dogmatic Constitution *Lumen gentium.*[5] In this document we are given the goal toward which every Christian in every state of life is called to journey. We share in a universal call to holiness. This call to holiness cannot effectively be heard unless we are in a heart-to-heart relationship with Christ.

Arminjon writes that the Song of Songs can be interpreted as a transparency of the love of God for creation and for his creatures. The biblical poem is ultimately about the absolute mystery of divine love. In the early history of the Church, several great spiritual writers perceived the Song of Songs as a marriage of God with His people and more specifically, of God with any soul seeking intimate union with Him. Fr. Arminjon mentions other spiritual giants, like St. Francis de Sales, who at the age of seventeen found this book to be so wonderfully evocative of God's desire to be close to our hearts. St. Therese of the Child Jesus, also at an early age, discovered the Song of Songs to be a profound explanation about a heart-to-heart relationship of love between the One who loves and the beloved. Of recent history, Cardinal Hans Urs von Balthasar commented that the Song of Songs has been a "secret sanctuary for the Church."[6]

How heart-to-heart conversation is nurtured:

Several years ago I heard a story which has influenced the way I pray the "Our Father." A group of pilgrims had made a trip to the Holy Land, and among the group was a priest who related

---

[4] Blaise Arminjon, S.J., *The Cantata of Love: A Verse by Verse Reading of the Song of Songs* (San Francisco, Ignatius Press, 1988).
[5] Marianne Lorraine Trouve, F.S.P., ed., "Lumen gentium," *The Sixteen Documents of Vatican II* (Boston: Pauline Books and Media, 1999) chapter 5.
[6] Arminjon, 39.

this story. He said the group stopped one afternoon by the Sea of Galilee and, while enjoying the sights and the good conversation, they noticed a boy in the lake who was struggling to stay above water. The boy's father dived into the water, positioned his own body underneath the boy's, and brought the boy up to safety. The little boy's response was to kiss his father over and over while calling "Abba, abba."

Jesus taught us to pray the "Our Father." For a biblical prayer to begin with "Father" is extraordinary. The Psalms, for example, are beautiful prayers, yet none of them addresses God in the way Jesus taught us. When Jesus used the term *abba* to refer to His Father, He was using the Aramaic language. The term evokes affection and tenderness, almost like a child referring to his father as *daddy*.

Heart-to-heart conversation with God our Father can be nurtured if we *pray as Jesus taught His disciples,* that is, if we pray the "Our Father" in the way Jesus used the term *abba*. When I pray the Lord's Prayer, quite often I have the mental image of the little boy safely sitting on his daddy's shoulders, kissing him and repeating the word *abba*.

True prayer allows for heart-to-heart conversation. The conversation might be with words, but oral expression is not a requirement. When two people speak from the heart, gestures and simple presence sometimes speak volumes. True prayer's heart-to-heart conversation allows me to realize that I am grounded in God and in God's Spirit. By virtue of my baptism the Holy Spirit dwells within me.

There are many methods of prayer which allow for heart-to-heart conversation. Here I shall describe two of them.

Lectio divina

One which comes to mind was acclaimed by Pope Benedict XVI early in his pontificate when he spoke about the beautiful practice of *lectio divina*. Addressing a number of biblical experts, the Pope urged a renewal of this ancient tradition and stated that if promoted correctly, it would bring a spiritual springtime to the Church.[7]

The steps for this method of prayer include reading the chosen Scripture passage, pondering it and trying to receive the full flavor of the passage, praying with the passage, contemplating the goodness of God, and finally giving room for the reflection of the passage to lead one to some form of action.

For example, in John 21:3 Simon Peter announces, "I am going fishing," and the other disciples chime back, "We also will come with you." They spend the night in the boat but catch nothing. The next morning, at dawn, Jesus calls to them, "Children, have you caught anything to eat?" They had not. Jesus then tells them to cast their net over the right side of the boat and they will catch something.

Using the method of *lectio divina*, I would first read the passage several times and try to envision as clearly as possible what is being said. After reading, it is helpful to spend a few moments pondering the passage. For example, the disciples were out all evening, but what about Jesus? Was He looking at them from the shore, keeping them in His sight and actually watching over them? What thoughts could have gone through Christ's mind as He watched them? Is there a reason why they were out in the boat without Him this time? Those are some of the ways we can ponder what we have read – almost like reading between the lines.

After pondering, we pray with the passage. For example: "Jesus, You promised to be with us always – even though we don't see Your physical presence. On those occasions when I am like the disciples who spent all night in the boat, I believe You are watching over me, too. Thank you, Jesus, for Your abiding presence and love."

---

[7] These remarks were given by Pope Benedict XVI on September 16, 2005, to the Catholic Biblical Federation and the Pontifical Council for Promoting Christian Unity who sponsored the international conference commemorating the fortieth anniversary of *Dei Verbum* from the Second Vatican Ecumenical Council.

Fourthly, we contemplate God's goodness. It is easy to see God's goodness in the Person of Jesus who tells the disciples to cast their nets on the right side of the boat. They receive more than they could ever have hoped for by their own strength or ingenuity.

Finally, in the fifth step we allow the passage to lead us to some form of action. Jesus, for example, was a gracious host after the fish were caught. He prepared the breakfast and asked them to "come and eat." Perhaps the passage will invite me to be more gracious in the way I treat others. Perhaps others will recognize the presence of Christ in me just as the disciples, after the invitation of Jesus to eat breakfast, realized that "it is the Lord."[8]

Colloquy

Another method for growth in prayer follows the method of Saint Ignatius of Loyola known as *colloquy*. In this method one's imagination is engaged by placing oneself within the Scripture passage being read. For example, using the Gospel passage of Peter walking toward Jesus on the water and placing myself in the picture, I might ask what I would have said had it been I walking on water instead of Peter. What would I have said had I been the first one to spot Jesus coming toward the boat? Had I been in the boat as one of Peter's companions, how would I have responded to Peter when he stepped out of the boat and onto the water? After Peter had his experience of walking on water, would I have wanted the same for myself? The purpose of this type of Ignatian prayer is to spend time in the company of Jesus. Ideally, this is the goal towards which all prayer strives – to spend time with Jesus and to let my heart envelop and be enveloped by Him.

---

[8] A helpful reference for a deeper understanding of *lectio divina* can be found in *Like the Deer That Yearns*, edited by Salvatore Panimolle (Petersham, Massachusetts: Saint Bede's Publications, 1998). This book draws upon several masters of spirituality who offer guidance in the art of careful listening to the Scriptures using the method of *lectio divina* which has been a part of the Church's treasury of prayer for centuries. The goal of this prayer form, according to Panimolle, is intimacy with God.

From the Catechism of the Catholic Church:

Part Four of the Catechism of the Catholic Church is devoted to prayer in the Christian life. As I have stated, I like to think of prayer as heart-to-heart conversation with God. We read about the heart in paragraph 2563:

> The heart is the dwelling-place where I am, where I live; according to the Semitic or Biblical expression, the heart is the place "to which I withdraw." The heart is our hidden center, beyond the grasp of the reason and of others; only the Spirit of God can fathom the human heart and know it fully. The heart is the place of decision, deeper than our psychic drives. It is the place of truth, where we choose life or death. It is the place of encounter, because as image of God we live in relation: it is the place of covenant.[9]

Reflection questions:

- Christ's heart is undivided in His love for me. Where do divisions exist in my heart with regard to my relationship with Christ?
- What do I need to do in order to overcome those divisions?
- Where will I start? When will I start?
- Peter's request that the Lord save him kept Peter from drowning. Was there a time in my life when I felt as though I were drowning? Did Peter's three words, "Lord, save me," also become my words?

> *A clean heart create for me, God;*
> *renew in me a steadfast spirit.*
> Ps 51:12

---

9 Catechism of the Catholic Church (Città del Vaticano: Libreria Editrice Vaticana, 1994).

Chapter 2

Reviewing the Influence of the Covenant Between God and Humanity

Scripture's insight:

Imagine that you and your friend, Cleopas, are the two disciples on the road to Emmaus (Lk 24:13-35). It is the very day Jesus has risen from the grave, and the events of the day have created quite a stir. You have been in Jerusalem throughout a good part of the day and now you are making the journey to Emmaus, about a seven-mile trip.

You and your companion are conversing about whether you believe Jesus really rose from the dead or whether this was the work of some devoted disciples, maybe even fanatic disciples, who wanted to feign a resurrection in order to counteract any further attempts by those who would want to discredit Jesus.

A question you might ask yourself as you journey to Emmaus is this: Why did you leave Jerusalem when you did? Apparently, you do not have the complete story about what occurred to Jesus. Did Jesus truly rise from the dead or not? Why didn't you stay to find out for sure – especially since this is a once-in-a-lifetime event? Are you and Cleopas afraid for your lives, thinking that the followers of Jesus might be persecuted in some way? Perhaps you simply want to get back home to your own family, to your spouse and children. Are you disillusioned because Jesus, the one whom most thought to be a political liberator, failed to overthrow the Roman government? Are you sad? Confused? Angry? Overcome with grief? Tired?

As you head toward Emmaus and are in conversation with Cleopas, you are joined by a third party. He is a bit intrusive to simply ask what you and Cleopas are talking about. However, you are both cordial and so you tell him about the events surrounding the crucifixion and the supposed resurrection of Jesus of Nazareth. What significant points do you include? The carrying of the cross? The sorrow of a mother holding the limp body of her son after being taken down from the cross? The sky turning dark because of the eclipse of the sun, or the veil of the temple being torn down at the same time Jesus hung upon the cross? The story given by the women about the resurrection of Jesus and how the disciples thought this story seemed like nonsense and so did not believe them? The fact that Peter went to the tomb and saw the burial cloths there, but the body was nowhere to be found?

The stranger lets you finish what you have to say about the events, and then says, "Was it not necessary that the Messiah should suffer these things and enter into his glory?" (v 26). Before you even have a chance to digest the question he has just posed, he begins to make reference to the Old Testament, recalling the covenant God made with Moses, the covenant God made with other prophets and leaders of the people, and finally the covenant God made with and in Jesus. Perhaps the words of this stranger about *covenant* are offering a bit of consolation to you, especially since you recall that some who were with Jesus at the Passover meal heard Him say, "This is the blood of the new and everlasting covenant that will be shed for you." As you and Cleopas and this stranger walk along, the idea of *covenant* remains with you.

You and Cleopas arrive at Emmaus as sunset approaches. Even though this stranger may have been somewhat intrusive in the beginning, you have taken a liking to him, so you ask him to stay the night with you since it is getting late. He gladly accepts and also takes you up on your offer of dinner.

Who comes to the dinner? Just you, Cleopas and the stranger? Do you have a family who join you? Does Cleopas have a family who also take part in the occasion? If family are present, how do you introduce the guest whom you have invited into your home? Listen! He is breaking the bread and saying the words of blessing. He offers you the bread, and as you take the offering, you look into his eyes. The *covenant!* Your own eyes have now been opened, you recognize that it is Jesus Himself; you see the wounds in His hands, and in an instant all the questions you had about the events of the past days are answered with crystal clarity. Before you can open your mouth to speak, He is gone. Evening or not, rough roads or not, tired or not, you and Cleopas set out on the seven-mile journey back to Jerusalem to report this awesome and wonderful encounter you had with the Risen Lord Jesus. I wonder whether you can even converse on the way back to Jerusalem or whether you are still awe-struck and speechless.

The insight of companions who experience the waters:
 In the Smithsonian Institute there is a diamond of deep blue color, almost 46 carats. It originated in India and was cut in the 17th century, having been owned by King Louis XIV of France for a time. A man named Hope purchased it; thus it is referred to as the Hope Diamond. Some believe this to be the most valuable jewel in all the world.

Pope John Paul II wrote the final encyclical of his pontificate in 2003. He wrote about what he considered the most valuable gift in all the world, but nowhere was the Hope Diamond mentioned. Rather, he referred to the gift of the Eucharist, the new and everlasting *covenant* of God's love concretized in the enduring presence of Jesus Christ. *Ecclesia de Eucharistia* (The Church of the Eucharist)[10] demonstrates beautifully how the great John Paul II appreciated the mystery of the covenant which is at the heart of every Eucharistic encounter. He writes:

> A *causal influence of the Eucharist* is present at the Church's very origins. The Evangelists specify that it was the Twelve, the Apostles, who gathered with Jesus at the Last Supper (cf. Mt 26:20; Mk 14:17; Lk 22:14). This is a detail of notable importance, for the Apostles "were both the seeds of the new Israel and the beginning of the sacred hierarchy." By offering them his body and his blood as food, Christ mysteriously involved them in the sacrifice which would be completed later on Calvary. By analogy with the Covenant of Mount Sinai, sealed by sacrifice and the sprinkling of blood, the actions and words of Jesus at

---
10 Pope John Paul II, *Ecclesia de Eucharistia* (Washington, D.C.: United States Conference of Catholic Bishops, 2003).

the Last Supper laid the foundations of the new messianic community, the People of the New Covenant.[11]

The covenant relationship between God and humanity is at the heart of sacred history. This covenant relationship is why we pray; it is why we are held in such tender care by our loving God. As the Catechism of the Catholic Church points out:

> Being in the image of God the human individual possesses the dignity of a person, who is not just something, but someone. He is capable of self-knowledge, of self-possession and of freely giving himself and entering into communion with other persons. And he is called by grace to a covenant with his Creator, to offer him a response of faith and love that no other creature can give in his stead.[12]

The notion of covenant carries with it a pledge between two parties for mutual assistance and support. Underlying the concept of covenant was the idea that both parties had something to offer in the deal. With covenants, rights were articulated and obligations were imposed. Interestingly, in the biblical accounts of covenant relationships, we are keenly aware of the inequality between God and humanity. Nevertheless, God initiates covenant relationships with His people. The Book of Genesis (2:16f) explains the covenant between God and Adam. Of course, man disobeyed and the covenant was broken. However, God's love is not severed and He promises to renew the covenant at a future point (3:15f).

God also entered into a covenant with Abraham and his posterity. This covenant was with the nation of Israel and, eventually, with all humanity. Israel's covenant with God is recorded in the Book of Isaiah (42:6). They, the people of Israel, are to be a light of revelation to all nations (cf. Catechism of the Catholic Church, 59-60). Ultimately, but after covenants with King David, Solomon, and others, the new and everlasting covenant which God establishes through Jesus Christ is truly the covenant which brings the "light

---

11 *Ibid.*, 22-23.
12 Catechism of the Catholic Church (Città del Vaticano: Libreria Editrice Vaticana, 1994) para. 357.

of revelation to the Gentiles, and glory for your people Israel" (Lk 2:32). Fr. Peter Stravinskas writes:

> The absoluteness and complete perfection of God's covenant with man reached perfection when it was made in Christ's blood for all people of all time (see Mk 14:23f; CCC 706). All former covenants found their fulfillment in this one covenant (Heb 8; CCC 1965ff). In his two beautiful canticles, Luke has Mary and Zechariah (1:46-55, 68-79) sing of the coming of Christ as the decisive event in the history of God's promises to Abraham and his descendants.[13]

How the influence of the covenant between God and humanity can be nurtured:

Earlier we addressed two forms of prayer, *lectio divina* and Ignatian prayer. These two methods exemplify ways to deepen heart-to-heart conversation. As we look now at the ways in which the covenant between God and humanity can be nurtured, a profound prayer form is the Eucharistic Prayer of the liturgy. The Eucharistic Prayer allows the praying assembly the opportunity to experience the covenant renewed. There are several approved Eucharistic prayer texts which the Catholic Church uses in her liturgy. The oldest Eucharistic Prayer dates back to about 215 A.D. and comes from the *Apostolic Tradition*. It is the Eucharistic Prayer of Hippolytus of Rome. The words of the institution narrative are:

> Before giving himself up to voluntary suffering in order to destroy death, to break the chains of the devil, to tread hell under his feet, to pour out his light upon the just, to establish the *Covenant* and manifest his Resurrection, he took bread, gave you thanks and said: "Take, eat, this is my body which is broken for you." The same way for the cup, he said: "This is my blood which is poured out for you. When you do this, do (it) in memory of me."[14]

---

[13] Peter M.J. Stravinskas, *The Catholic Church and the Bible* (San Francisco: Ignatius Press, 1996) 35.
[14] Lucien Deiss, *The Mass* (Collegeville, Minnesota: Liturgical Press, 1992) 65.

In the Eucharistic Prayer the assembly prays *Hosanna,* which literally means "Give salvation." This is the new and everlasting Covenant; this is the work of Jesus Christ. Time spent in prayer, whether alone or with the gathered assembly in the Eucharistic celebration, is an opportunity for us to cry out *Hosanna!*

In the Eucharistic Prayer we hear the words of Jesus, "This is my Body; this is my Blood." In the Eucharist, Jesus truly gives us His Body, the whole of His life from the first moment of the Incarnation and everything He experienced during His life. In the Eucharist, Jesus truly gives us His Blood, the essence of His life. In the Eucharistic Prayer, the Holy Spirit substantially changes the bread and wine so that they become the Body and Blood, Soul and Divinity of Christ. In that sense, the Spirit cries, *"Maranatha,* come, Lord Jesus!" It is the Lord Jesus, seated at the right hand of the Father forever, who also is present upon the altar in what had previously been bread and wine. It is Christ's Body, Blood, Soul and Divinity which are present in the Sacred Host.

Likewise, the gathered assembly, the Church as bride of Christ, cries in the same Holy Spirit, "Come, Lord Jesus." We call upon the Spirit to nourish us so that we can better represent the Mystical Body of Christ in the world, and, by virtue of our baptism, can be the presence of Christ to others. In a sense, during the Mass, the presence of Jesus is something we can best appreciate by remembering that He is in heaven, He is truly present in the consecrated bread and wine, and He is present in the body of believers who are united in the Holy Spirit. This new and everlasting covenant, given by God out of love for us, allows our *Hosanna* as well as our *Amen* to be a heartfelt response to God's divine initiative.

In reviewing the influence of the covenant between God and humanity, we would do well to recall our baptism. We were baptized in order to enter into a covenant with God. As we celebrate the new and everlasting covenant in the Eucharistic Prayer, we can remember that this "new" covenant replaces all former covenants.

The covenant with Moses serves as an example. In Exodus 24 we read how Moses proclaimed God's Word, sprinkled the blood of immolated lambs over the people, and then ate and drank. These actions had symbolic meaning in terms of the relationship the people of Israel wanted with God. The Catholic celebration of the Holy Eucharist with the beautiful prayer renewing the "new and everlasting covenant" speaks the same sentiment; it is the source and the summit of all humanity's relationship with God.

When I think of how this covenant between God and humanity can be better nurtured, I try to remember the words of Jesus to His disciples as they prepared to share the Passover Meal on the night before He died. Jesus said, "I have eagerly desired to eat this Passover with you before I suffer" (Lk 22:15). These words of Jesus remind me that *He* is the one who wants me to come to the Eucharist, to come to the Eucharistic covenant ceremony which we call the Holy Sacrifice of the Mass. It is Jesus who wants to share the meal with me and who wants me to receive His life which is for the salvation of the world.

I try to offer this thought when someone says, "I don't get anything out of the Mass." I bristle a bit. "What do you mean, you don't *get* anything out of the Mass? You *get* to share in the heavenly banquet Jesus is offering you — His own Body and Blood. You *get* the love, mercy, and forgiveness this covenant offers. You *get* to be as close to God as anyone can get. Finally, you *get* the opportunity to grow in grace and be part of the Mystical Body of Christ."

What else do we get at the Eucharist? We *get* to *give* a response to the God of the Universe who truly **wants** to spend time with us. We *get* to eat, drink, pray, and love in memory of the Christ, the anointed of God.

"Christ has no hands but your hands, no feet but yours." These words remind us how we continue the work of Christ; the mystery of the Incarnation continues through the community of disciples who form their lives around Christ as Head. The continuing work of the Incarnation is perhaps best recognized at the Mass, the covenant celebration of the Holy Eucharist, where the real presence of Christ is known:

1) Jesus is eternally in heaven and is seated at the right hand of the Father, but

2) Jesus is also in the consecrated bread and wine which become His Body, Blood, Soul and Divinity, and

3) Jesus is in the community of believers who conform their lives to His and in a particular way through the priest (a member of the community of believers who at that moment acts in the person of Christ the Head) who lends Jesus his mouth so that Jesus can speak the words, "This is my body ... this is my blood."

From the Catechism of the Catholic Church:

Previously we examined how prayer is a heart-to-heart encounter. The Catechism of the Catholic Church ties together the two themes, the heart and the covenant, as we have already examined: "The heart is the place of decision, deeper than our psychic drives. It is the place of truth, where we choose life or death. It is the place of encounter, because as image of God we live in relation: it is the place of covenant." (CCC 2563) In paragraph 2564 we read further:

> Christian prayer is a covenant relationship between God and man in Christ. It is the action of God and of man, springing forth from both the Holy Spirit and ourselves, wholly directed to the Father, in union with the human will of the Son of God made man.

Finally, the covenant theme which reveals God's favor (grace) is summarized in paragraph 2565:

> In the New Covenant, prayer is the living relationship of the children of God with the Father who is good beyond measure, with his Son Jesus Christ and with the Holy Spirit. The grace of the Kingdom is "the union of the entire holy and royal Trinity ... with the whole human spirit." Thus, the life of prayer is the habit of being in the presence of the thrice-holy God and in communion with him. This communion of life is always possible because, through Baptism, we have already been united with Christ. Prayer is *Christian* insofar as it is communion with Christ and extends

throughout the Church, which is his Body. Its dimensions are those of Christ's love.

Reflection questions:
- Is it possible for me to see my life as part of the covenant relationship God has established with all of humanity?
- If not, what hinders me from realizing this?
- If there are hindrances, might there be some helpful steps I should take in order to move more fully into the covenant relationship?
- If I do consider my life as part of God's covenant relationship, what obligations do I have? What might God be expecting of me?
- What are the rights God has given to me?
- What do I, in turn, expect from God?
- At Mass, when I pray "Lord, I am not worthy to receive You; only say the word and I shall be healed," am I able to enter deeply into the reality of the covenant which God has initiated with me?

> *He remembers forever his covenant,*
> *the pact imposed for a thousand generations,*
> *Which was made with Abraham,*
> *confirmed by oath to Isaac,*
> *And ratified as binding for Jacob,*
> *an everlasting covenant for Israel.*
> Ps 105:8-10

Chapter 3

Accepting the Water from Jesus

Scripture's insight:

Some might call it a chance meeting, but this is hardly the case since the encounters with Christ in the Scriptures are timely and even urgent. The Samaritan woman was confronted by the fullness of truth when she met Jesus that noonday at the well. She gradually untangled the strands of her life as she realized what Christ's water could provide. The grace of God was at work in her, and Jesus showed the depth of understanding while never backing away from calling her to truth and accountability. Beneath the truth of her sins lay the recognition of her goodness, and Jesus encouraged this Samaritan woman to drink plentifully from the water He could provide.

This intriguing passage is found in the Gospel according to John (4:4-42). It exemplifies the attitude of Jesus. He shows care and compassion; He shows that His life is exquisite and plentiful; He shows truth and healing. For our part, all we need to do is come to Him and accept the water He offers.

John's Gospel develops a theology of salvation by recalling that faith in the Son of God brings eternal life, while disobeying Him brings "God's wrath" (3:36). The Samaritan woman, her kinsmen, as well as the Galilean and Judaean Jews, are among those who are the "fruit for eternal life" (4:36). The Samaritan woman and the townsfolk awaken to a deeper understanding of Jesus, and their attitude becomes more closely attuned to the attitude of Christ. They recognize Him first as a Jew (4:9), then as a prophet (4:19), then as the Christ (4:25-26, 29), and finally, as Savior of the world (4:42). Not only do they recognize Him, but they also go the next step – they *accept* what He offers.

Jesus calmly rebukes the Samaritan woman's adulterous relationships and, in so doing, invites her to accept conversion. She listens to Him and believes that Jesus is the prophet. She leaves her water jar behind as she heads off to proclaim to others what she has encountered in Jesus. The water jar might represent her former lifestyle which she now leaves behind since she has drunk from the water of life (4:14). She no longer needs to fill the water jar with water that will satisfy only for a short duration; she has experienced the life-giving water, and her attitude – her very life – has been altered. She has accepted the water from Jesus.

History suggests that the relationship between the Samaritans and Jews was one of antagonism and sharp division. We can assume the Samaritan woman would have been quite surprised to have a Jew (Jesus) speak to her. He was even willing to drink from the water jar she carried before suggesting to her what He could offer.

The water jar is significant. Women would carry water jars on their backs and might make the trip from the village to the well several times a day. After a period of time, one might have a twisted back from the constant weight of the jar and its contents. This woman of Samaria may have had a twisted back; she certainly had a twisted view of life as she deviated from God's plan for marriage. Nevertheless, Jesus drank from her jar and then spoke to her about the life-giving water He could give. She thirsted for that water, and indeed, she drank. All the while, she was advancing in the attitude Christ wanted for her, the attitude of love.

The Samaritan woman invites her neighbors to "come and see a man who told me everything I've done!" (4:29). She piques their curiosity when she asks aloud whether He could be the Messiah. In the Gospel according to John, we often find this theme of accepting the water of Jesus by means of a personal decision of faith. The Samaritan woman decided in faith that Jesus was indeed Savior (4:42), thus capturing the essence of 3:16, revealing Christ as salvation for all who call upon Him. The Samaritan woman was gradually led to faith because she was receptive to the water Jesus could provide. Her faith changed her – and brought her to salvation. In so doing, she 1) heard the truth of God in Jesus' words, 2) experienced in Jesus' actions the attitude of loving compassion, and

3) laid down her water jar, laid down her sin, and instead accepted the Living Water whose name is Jesus.

The insight of companions who experience the waters:

Anyone who has heard the preaching of Fr. John Corapi, a member of the Society of Our Lady of the Most Holy Trinity, knows of the great possibility for conversion in one's life. Hearing Fr. Corapi's life story also inspires the hearer to realize that accepting the water from Jesus is usually a step-by-step process.

Fr. Corapi's story, as he tells it, is about a man who wanted to "be somebody." He did not find what he was looking for in high school athletics nor as part of the Green Berets during the time of the Vietnam War. He did not find what he was looking for as an accountant, living in the fast lane and growing very wealthy. He did not find the "somebody" he wanted to be through his association with famous celebrities or with his expensive and lavish lifestyle. He did not find what he was looking for when he became involved with cocaine and nearly died from his heavy use of the substance. Only when he felt as though he were in absolute darkness was he able to climb up from the depths of despair surrounding him. His story reminds us of God's grace. After having been away from the Church for many years, John Corapi returned one day to receive the sacrament of reconciliation. The floodgates of God's mercy opened – and the rest of the story takes us to Fr. Corapi's ordination to the priesthood, his outstanding ability to bring God's message of love by means of his preaching, and his desire to lead souls to the wellspring of life, Jesus.

To grow in holiness, to grow in the attitude of Christ, one needs to foster those things which allow for an ever-deepening and uncompromising love for Jesus, for the Church Christ founded, and for the teachings the Magisterium of the Church has given to us. Fr. Corapi, like the Samaritan woman of the Gospel story, experienced the compassionate love of Jesus, allowed Christ to shape his own attitude, and laid down the burden of sin in order to take up more dutifully the cross of Christ.

Conversion experiences in which one symbolically lays down the water jar are part of the story of Scripture. One need only consider Saint Paul, the Apostle to the Gentiles, who initially had a hand in the persecution of Christians. However, the compassionate love of Jesus touched him and he was forever changed.

The compassionate love of Jesus is freely offered to everyone. As Pope Benedict XVI states in his encyclical *Deus Caritas Est:* "This God loves man."[15] He continues his reflection of love by reminding us:

> The one God in whom Israel believes ... loves with a personal love. His love, moreover, is an elective love: Among all the nations he chooses Israel and loves her – but he does so precisely with a view to healing the whole human race.[16]

The message of Pope Benedict XVI is one of hope. It is a reminder that in Christ we have the fullness of redemption. Our attitude can be shaped by the love of Jesus. The Holy Father's encyclical reminds Christians that unless we come to know God as the one who loves us, unless we come to know the Son of God as Truth who loves us, we fail to grasp what is at the heart of Christianity. This love, evident throughout the Scriptures and certainly shown in the case of the Samaritan woman, is described in this way by Pope Benedict XVI:

> God's passionate love for his people – for humanity – is at the same time a forgiving love. It is so great that it turns God against himself, his love against his justice. Here Christians can see a dim prefigurement of the mystery of the cross: So great is God's love for man that by becoming man he follows him even into death, and so reconciles justice and love.[17]

We advance in the attitude of Christ as we would grow in any intimate love relationship. It requires intimacy rather than a casual

---

15 Pope Benedict XVI, *Deus Caritas Est, Origins* 35:33 (February 2, 2006) 545.
16 *Ibid.*
17 *Ibid.*

acquaintance. Further, it requires trust and surrender, first a trust that our defenses can be lowered without feeling shame, and then a surrender of our very selves. What is necessary in this process is humility which allows us to be open to the love and the transforming goodness of Christ, a humility which leaves us vulnerable ultimately to the God who intimately loves every woman and man and offers life-giving water.

One individual who comes to mind as I think about advancing in the attitude of Christ and accepting Jesus' life-giving water is a recently-canonized saint of the Catholic Church, Saint Gianna Beretta Molla. Only within the last several years have I learned about the heroic virtue of Saint Gianna Beretta Molla. I now pray to her each day and ask her intercession to help all of us, especially Catholics, to understand the value of human life from the moment of conception.

Saint Gianna died in 1962, following the birth of her fourth child. She was declared a saint in May of 2004 by Pope John Paul II. Her husband, Pietro, was present for his wife's canonization ceremony in Rome.

Gianna Beretta (1922-1962) grew up in a devout Catholic family with twelve siblings. When she was a teenager, her older sister died, and this had a profound influence on Gianna. At that point she desired to deepen her relationship with Christ. Her desire was the impetus she needed in order to begin her true advancement in the attitude of Christ. She joined an association of young Catholics called Catholic Action which stressed Eucharistic devotion, apostolic action, and heroic purity. Even at this early age, she was convinced of the necessity and the effectiveness of prayer. It was in the Catholic Action association that she met her future husband, Pietro Molla.

As a young adult Gianna completed her medical studies and began her work as a physician, specializing in pediatrics. She and Pietro married in 1955, living so beautifully the words of Sacred Scripture that speak about the two becoming one. Her desire was to allow her marriage to be the vocation leading her to holiness. Of her vocation to marriage she wrote: "God has shown each one of us the way, the vocation, and the life of grace that lies beyond physical life. Our earthly and eternal happiness depends on following our vocation without faltering. What is a vocation? It is a gift from God."[18]

In 1961, at the beginning of Gianna's fourth pregnancy, she discovered she had a cyst on the wall of her uterus. Doctors recommended removal of the cyst and abortion of the child. Gianna and Pietro would not consider abortion for any reason. The cyst was removed, but the child in her womb was given every opportunity to grow. The child was delivered by Caesarean section, but within the week, Gianna had died resulting from complications. Those who were at her side in the final moments of her earthly life heard her saying, "Jesus, I love you; Jesus, I love you."

There are couples who wish to conceive a child and find themselves unable to do so. As devotion to Saint Gianna is increasingly known, couples are asking her intercession. In some cases, this has resulted in the conception and birth of a child. Saint Gianna Beretta Molla reminds me that by accepting Jesus and His life-giving water into her own life, she not only advanced in the attitude of Jesus Christ but also furthered Christ's Kingdom on earth. Indeed, she is one of the great Christian pray-ers.

How advancing in the attitude of Christ can be nurtured:

A Cherokee proverb has been handed down over the years, suggesting that on a certain evening one of the great Cherokee elders told his grandson about a battle raging inside each person. He said, "My son, the battle is between two 'wolves' that live inside all of us. One is evil: it is anger, envy, jealousy, greed, arrogance, self-pity, resentment, lies, false pride, superiority and ego. The other good: it is joy, peace, love, hope, serenity, humility, kindness, empathy, truth, compassion and faith."

---

18 Giuliana Pelucchi, *Blessed Gianna Beretta Molla: A Woman's Life* (Boston: Pauline Books and Media, 2002) 71.

The grandson thought about this for a minute and then asked his grandfather, "Which wolf wins?" The Cherokee elder replied, "The one you feed."

It does not come as a surprise to us to know that within each human person there is the potential for both good and evil. None of us is exempt from the temptation to sin. It is Christ and the attitude of Christ which can help us to move toward a kind of indifference, not allowing ourselves to entertain thoughts which feed the evil wolf. The indifference is not an indifference to sin; rather, it is an indifference of attitude we acquire toward the temptation so we do not welcome it into our thoughts.

In the Eucharistic celebration we are fed with life-giving Bread. If we have received the life-giving Bread appropriately, then we grow in the virtuous life. We grow in joy, peace, love, hope, and the other virtues. The focus of our prayer during the liturgy is the community's worship of God the Father through the Son and in the Holy Spirit. We join in this prayer to the Father through, with, and in Christ. Our prayer is one of adoration, and adoration is necessary in order for us to sustain a proper relationship of love for God. Likewise, we cannot truly love Christ without adoring Him. A privileged way to love Christ and to adore Him is in adoration of the Blessed Sacrament. In adoration of Christ we are able to ask the Lord to help us grow in His attitude. "Let your attitude be that of Christ" is what Saint Paul taught. Adoration of Christ allows the attitude of Christ to grow within us. When this happens, we are making a decision about which wolf to feed.

During the Mass our adoration is primarily directed toward God the Father; in Eucharistic adoration outside of Mass, our focus is directed primarily toward God the Son. It becomes a wonderful time to take the words of Saint Peter to heart: "Come to him, a living stone, rejected by human beings but chosen and precious in the sight of God, and, like living stones, let yourselves be built into a spiritual house to be a holy priesthood to offer spiritual sacrifices acceptable to God through Jesus Christ" (1 Pt 2:4).

The Catholic Church teaches that adoration of Christ in the Blessed Sacrament must always be understood as deriving from the Real Presence of Jesus, the Christ, in the actual celebration of the Eucharist. Therefore, adoration begins in the Mass itself. While the main focus of adoration during the Eucharist is toward God the Father, there are specific moments when adoration of Christ occurs as well.

Anyone who tries to understand what takes place during the Mass realizes that the mystery is truly unfathomable. We can never fully understand what great love prompted God's divine intervention on our behalf. Adoration of Jesus in the Blessed Sacrament outside of Mass gives us an extended opportunity to enter into contemplation of the mystery of God's love for us.

In the early Church, Eucharistic adoration as we know it today had not yet developed, so reservation of the Eucharist was allowed primarily so that those who could not attend Mass (such as the sick) would still be able to receive Communion. Implicit in this practice is the understanding that Christ's presence in the Eucharist remains beyond the time of the actual liturgical celebration. This understanding is also the basis for the second aspect of reserving the Blessed Sacrament: to adore Christ who is really present in the consecrated Host. Spending time with Christ in the devotional practice of Eucharistic adoration allows one to appreciate all the more the heavenly meal Jesus desired to share with His disciples. Also, spending time before the Blessed Sacrament in adoration of Jesus allows one to experience what the disciples on the road to Emmaus received – a greater understanding of the Scriptures, which caused their hearts to burn within them.

From the Catechism of the Catholic Church:
The passage from Scripture upon which we have reflected briefly allowed us to meet the Samaritan woman at the well. Beginning with a quote from John's Gospel dealing with the Samaritan woman, the Catechism of the Catholic Church offers a salient summary of Christ's interaction with the woman (who can easily symbolize all of humanity) and of her growth in the attitude of Christ:

"If you knew the gift of God!" (Jn 4:10). The wonder of prayer is revealed beside the well where we come seeking water: there, Christ comes to meet every human being. It is he who first seeks us and asks us for a drink. Jesus thirsts; his asking arises from the depths of God's desire for us. Whether we realize it or not, prayer is the encounter of God's thirst with ours. God thirsts that we may thirst for him.[19]

The final sentence of the paragraph reflects the thought of St. Augustine. This thought is evidenced in the Gospel when Jesus asks the woman for a drink. Jesus, God Himself, experienced thirst in that moment. As the woman offered Jesus a drink, she opened herself to the dialogue which would invite her to thirst for Him.

Another time when Jesus experienced thirst was when He hung upon the cross and cried out, "I thirst." When we as Christians remember the sacrifice of Christ on Calvary because of His love for the Father and the Father's children, we, like the Samaritan woman, are able to open ourselves to a dialogue with Jesus that would invite us to thirst for Him as well.

Reflection questions:
- What is the water jar I might leave behind as I accept the invitation of Jesus to drink from His living water?
- Has carrying the water jar distorted my life in any way?
- In what ways is God thirsting so that I might thirst for Him?
- How fully do I accept Pope Benedict XVI's statement that God's love for His people is *passionate*?
- Can I make a connection between the Holy Father's statement and the *Passion* of Jesus?
- Am I able to see how Eucharistic adoration outside of Mass allows me to extend in time and in contemplation the mystery which occurs at Mass when the priest elevates the consecrated Host?

---
19 Catechism of the Catholic Church, para. 2560.

- Can I appreciate Eucharistic adoration as an extended meditation on the words "Lord, I am not worthy ... only say the word and I shall be healed" which we pray at Mass?

> *O God, you are my God –*
> *for you I long!*
> *For you my body yearns;*
> *for you my soul thirsts.*
> Ps. 63:2

Chapter 4

Yearning for the Fire of the Holy Spirit

Scripture's insight:

The two disciples to whom Jesus had appeared after His resurrection hurried from Emmaus to Jerusalem to tell the other disciples about what had occurred. They recounted the events of their amazing story. The disciples were still speaking about this when "he stood in their midst and said to them, 'Peace be with you'"(Lk 24:36). He then asked if they had anything to eat, and He received baked fish. He spoke further, opening their eyes and hearts to the teachings of Moses and the prophets, and He showed them how the Psalms they had so often recited needed to be fulfilled. He helped them to understand the Scriptures – how, for example, the Messiah would suffer and rise from the dead, and how repentance for the forgiveness of sins would be preached in the Messiah's name. Then came the zinger: "You are witnesses of these things" (v 48). After that, the final word: "And behold I am sending the promise of my Father upon you" (v 49).

The "promise of my Father" refers to the Holy Spirit. The disciples heard Jesus tell them that this promise was going to be sent to them, actually sent upon them. Then He went with them to Bethany where He blessed them and was taken from their midst. They went back to Jerusalem, probably with many mixed emotions.

The promise Jesus spoke about brings us to the conclusion of Luke's Gospel. The promise is also the beginning of the Acts of the Apostles, sometimes referred to as the Gospel of the Holy Spirit and often considered to be authored by Luke. The author of the Acts of the Apostles reminds us that the final words of Jesus before His ascension were to encourage the disciples and to instruct them that they would "receive power when the Holy Spirit comes upon you" (1:6). The power of the Spirit would give them courage to be His witnesses.

How many disciples were gathered together? Where did this gathering occur – in whose house? What were they doing when the noise began and the driving wind filled the house? What we do know is that the promise of Jesus had now been fulfilled. The courage which the disciples needed to be witnesses to Christ's resurrection and to the wonderful message of the forgiveness of sins had been given. Additionally, the Spirit was not only given to the disciples who were gathered together but was also to be given to all who would "repent and be baptized ... in the name of Jesus Christ" (2:38). Things would never be the same again.

The insight of companions who experience the waters:

What comes to mind when entertaining thoughts about the Holy Spirit? The image of fire is common and quite often associated with the tongues of fire resting upon the heads of the disciples. Sometimes the depiction will be seven tongues of fire, representing the gifts of the Holy Spirit described in Isaiah 11:2-3. Prayers to the Holy Spirit also make reference to "kindling the fire of divine love."

It was Saint Irenaeus, born in the first half of the second century, chosen as a bishop and declared a Father of the Church, who wrote a number of treatises against heretical teachings, one of which dealt with the Person of the Holy Spirit. Irenaeus spoke of the Holy Spirit in terms of water and moisture. He also indicated that the Holy Spirit, given at Pentecost after the Lord's ascension, made known to human beings the new covenant – i.e., the covenant that we now have in Jesus Christ. His insights are tremendous and worthy of our meditation:

> This was why the Lord had promised to send the Advocate: he was to prepare us as an offering to God. Like dry flour, which cannot become one lump of dough, one loaf of bread, without moisture, we who are many could not become one in Christ Jesus without the water that comes down from heaven. And like parched ground, which yields no harvest unless it receives moisture, we who were once like a waterless tree could never have lived and borne fruit without this abundant rainfall from above. Through the baptism that liberates us from change and decay we have become one in body; through the Spirit we have become one in soul.[20]

---

20 Saint Irenaeus, *Adversus haereses*. This is a treatise by Saint Irenaeus in five

The writings of Saint Irenaeus reflect very beautifully the theology of the Holy Spirit as Advocate "to prepare us as an offering to God." The Holy Spirit, then, is a Divine Person of the Blessed Trinity. The Father created us, the Son redeemed us, and the Holy Spirit continues to sanctify us as helper and advocate for the glory of God the Father, for our good and for the good of all the Church (cf. 1 Pt 1:2).

When do we most experience the presence of God? He is the God whom we call the "Lord and giver of life" when we profess the Nicene Creed. The answer will vary for each individual. Parents frequently say that childbirth is one of those times. The image of childbirth reminds us that not every birth is an easy process. As a matter of fact, not every child's birth is joyful. An example I think of is when my nephew was born. It was not known until his birth that his heart was severely defective. Moments after birth he was rushed to a major medical facility where in the ensuing days, two extensive operations were performed. Unfortunately, the baby did not survive. I remember being in the room with my sister as she held the lifeless body of her son; almost in shock she kept repeating, "Did this happen because I am not a good mother?"

I use this example because the presence of the Holy Spirit is not only for the joyful moments of life. Childbirth, the example we are using, can be a joyful time or a time which presents the harsh reality of death. Either way, the Spirit is present and gives life. It may be a different kind of life than the one we were anticipating. Nevertheless, the creative work of the Spirit allows us to call Him "Lord and giver of life."

A beautiful prayer of the Catholic tradition is the *Anima Christi* (Soul of Christ) which dates back to about the 14th century. It begins: "Soul of Christ, sanctify me. Body of Christ, save me. Blood of Christ, inebriate me." The verb *inebriate* is powerful. Quite often we associate the word with someone who has consumed an excessive amount of alcohol. However, that is a very limited use

---

books, devoted to "The Detection and Overthrow of False Knowledge." The cited paragraph comes from Book 3, ch. 2.

of the word. From a spiritual point of view, we might consider those virtuous souls who were drunk with a love for God, a thirst that could not be quenched no matter how much they imbibed of God's grace. Inebriation usually leads us to think of exhilaration and enjoyment; all the more in the spiritual sense! The person who wants to become inebriated by the love of Christ is one who finds his or her relationship with Christ to be exhilarating and fulfilling. How beautiful to think of a relationship with Christ as enjoyable – and one who thinks like that has understood the spiritual dimension of inebriation.

The Acts of the Apostles tell us that, on the first Pentecost day, Peter and the others were speaking to the crowds with exhilaration. As a matter of fact, someone even said, "They have had too much new wine" (2:13). Peter, along with the Eleven standing with him, responded, "These people are not drunk, as you suppose, for it is only nine o'clock in the morning" (2:14). One type of inebriation was insinuated; a deeper inebriation had taken hold of the Apostles. They were filled with the Spirit, the presence of Christ until the end of time. Mother Mary Francis, P.C.C., writes the following of this event:

> They were inebriated with the blood of Christ, whose effects the Holy Spirit was at that moment bringing to climactic action. And whenever we are enabled by the Holy Spirit to exceed ourselves, to surpass our natural capabilities, we are experiencing in our measure and expressing within our possibilities the inebriation that is the effect of the blood of Christ outpoured.[21]

How yearning for the fire of the Holy Spirit can be nurtured:

The promise Jesus made to His disciples was an assurance that the Holy Spirit would give them courage to be His witnesses. The same Holy Spirit, offering the same courage, is the very same promise which the Risen Lord Jesus gives to those who repent and who are baptized in the name of Jesus (cf. Acts 2:38).

---

21 Mother Mary Francis, P.C.C., *Anima Christi: Soul of Christ* (San Francisco: Ignatius Press, 2001) 32.

How can we nurture the desire to have the fire of the Spirit burn within us? In the prayer "Come, Holy Spirit," the answer is given. The prayer concludes with this thought:

*O God, who by the light of the Holy Spirit, did instruct the hearts of the faithful, grant us in the same Spirit to be **truly wise and ever to rejoice in His consolation.***

We yearn for the fire of the Holy Spirit when we seek true wisdom and when we rejoice in the Spirit's consolation. Perhaps an example will help.

When I was in grade school, seventh grade to be exact, I was given a holy card by a priest from a missionary community. He wanted me to consider attending their high school seminary, but I had no desire. The holy card was dutifully tucked away and used as a bookmark in my Bible.

Years later, while trying to discern whether I had a call to the priesthood, I looked at the holy card as if for the first time. The words on the card said, "How can I best serve You?" As I prayed those words in the days and months to follow, I was seeking true wisdom.

I was ordained to the priesthood in 1978. While I believe that my vocation was and is the grace of seeking *true wisdom*, it was only later that I also felt the importance of seeking the grace of *courage*, perhaps the kind of courage about which we read in the Acts of the Apostles.

On May 13, 1981, there occurred the assassination attempt on the life of Pope John Paul II. Along with many throughout the world, I prayed for his recovery. I then realized that when Karol Cardinal Wojtyla accepted the election to the papacy, it must have occurred to him that his life could be ended in an instant by those who might wish to silence him. It was the assassination attempt on the Pope's life which led me to further reflection about the courage he demonstrated at different stages of his life.

The assassination attempt on the life of the Holy Father also led me to deeper reflection and prayer about what kind of courage I possessed – or more realistically, the courage I did not possess. I have prayed since to the Holy Spirit for the gift of true courage. The question up to this point had been, "How can I best serve You?" The new question became, "What am I willing to die for?"

I remember viewing the movie *The Mission*, which was produced in 1986. The story is about several Spanish Jesuits who tried to protect a South American Indian tribe from a pro-slavery ruling government. For me, the most inspirational part of the movie was when the priest and villagers courageously carried the Eucharist in the midst of conflict, knowing that bloodshed and death would probably be the outcome. He, the priest, was willing to die for the people he hoped to help, and he was willing to die for Christ, truly present in the Eucharist he carried. I left the movie with a lump in my throat. The image of the priest who carried the sacramental Christ (the Eucharist) in procession as a protection for the mystical Christ (the indigenous tribe) left me with one question – what would I do?

I hope I am willing to die for Christ and for the Church. More importantly, I want to live for the same. In prayer each day, I continue to ask the Lord for true wisdom and courage. Those individuals whose courageous lives have blessed my own continue to be a great source of strength and their friendship provides consolation. The words of St. Basil the Great come to mind: "But we must care about truth, not our own safety."[22] So how do we yearn for the fire of the Holy Spirit? Pray for it – pray for true wisdom and courage, for reverence and right judgment, for any and all of the gifts which the Holy Spirit is only too "ready and willing" to offer us.

Another way in which we can yearn for the fire of the Holy Spirit is to begin each day with the gentle reminder that God is asking us to serve Him. God wants us to know, love, and serve Him. The practical aspect of this kind of service is that we renounce the

---

22 St. Basil the Great, *On the Holy Spirit* (Crestwood, New York: St. Vladimir's Seminary Press, 1980) 81.

evil in the world and all around us. As we renounce evil, the fire of the Holy Spirit will surely intensify.

Non serviam – I will not serve. This is the response of evil in the face of good. The Book of Genesis states that all of God's creation was good. God is the Author of all that is good and only that which is good. Whence evil? Evil is the opposite of good, the lack of good, that which is contrary to good. The personification of evil is not difficult to comprehend; we need only be reminded of some of the most evil atrocities committed in the history of humankind and there we will find evil. We associate evil with people like Hitler, Stalin, bin Laden and Hussein. We do so because these and others epitomize the opposite of goodness as they murdered hundreds and thousands of people under their dictatorships. Evil exists in varying degrees and with varying levels of intensity.

Beginning with baptism, and every time we renew our baptismal vows, we are asked, "Do you renounce evil?" Of course, anyone committed to Christian discipleship will answer affirmatively. "Do you renounce Satan and all his empty works and all his empty promises?" Some have difficulty with the reality of Satan or with even the concept of the devil. (The little red guy, pitchfork in hand, long tail and horns protruding from his head, is an image best left for the cartoons.) Satan, however, is as real and even more evil than the worst of humans with whom we associate the concept of evil. Satan's goal is to attract the beautiful human beings that are part of God's good creation. His intent is to bring humans down to his level, turning our backs on God and rejecting God's faithfulness. Ultimately, Satan wants to destroy the credibility of Jesus Christ in the world today, for Jesus is the most concrete sign of God's loving fidelity.

A priest for whom I had great respect was a Capuchin friar, Fr. Louis Biersack. Before his death I had been told Fr. Louis would never speak an unkind word about anyone. Wow! After hearing this about Fr. Louis, I asked him once what he thought about the devil. Fr. Louis' response was succinct: "Well, he's patient." True to form, Fr. Louis did not speak an unkind word – even about the devil.

Also true to form, the devil's patience may simply be a ploy to numb us so that eventually we become unresponsive to the evil around us. Evil becomes so commonplace that after a while, the horror of the evil fades away. Another ploy of the devil is to make us think he is not real. When we do not notice him, he can work all the more effectively. Fr. Louis was right; the devil is patient.

The reason many reject the idea of a devil is because, as in the case of an angel, we are speaking of pure spirit. Since we cannot see these pure spirits – neither good nor evil ones – some choose to deny their existence. Simply because I may choose to reject these creatures does not mean that their existence is not real. They are present and they are real. Today these pure spirits are saying to God either *serviam* (the angel) or *non serviam* (the devil). For them there is no turning back from their original decision to serve or not to serve God.

Non serviam was the response made by those angels who opposed God, who opposed God's goodness. Angels, like humans, have been given free will. Unlike humans, the fallen angels have not been redeemed. God has chosen the gift of redemption and salvation for the part of creation a degree lower than the angels. He has chosen the gift of redemption for us. Like the fallen angels who opposed God's total goodness, therefore choosing the totality of evil, we have been given the choice to serve God or not to serve God.

Unlike the fallen angels, we have opportunities to change from *non serviam* to *serviam* right up to the moment of our final breath. Because of God's special love for humanity, we are given opportunity time and again to turn away from evil and be faithful to the goodness of God. We can be faithful to the Gospel, the good news of God's love for us in Jesus Christ. The daily reminder that we will serve God and will renounce evil allows the fire of the Spirit to deepen in our hearts.

The rite of baptism is demonstrably the sacrament most often associated with the image of water. Water is used in varying degrees (pouring over the head of the one to be baptized versus a total immersion into a pool of water) and reminds us of Jesus' own baptism in the Jordan River by John. In the baptismal ceremony we are also reminded of water's usage in key moments of salvation history: the parting of the Red Sea by Moses and then the subsequent return of the waters which destroyed Pharaoh's charioteers, the water from the rock which the Israelites were given, ultimately leading us to consider the blood and water flowing from Jesus' side as He hung upon the cross.

My mother used to bless my two sisters and me with holy water every night before we went to bed. She was also lavish in blessing our home with holy water. She believed that this sacramental, holy water, was powerful. Of course, she was right. There are miraculous springs of water, Lourdes, for example, which remind us of water's power. The waters of baptism are not ordinary; they lead to salvation. There's power in that water! Jesus told His disciples to baptize in the name of the Father, and of the Son, and of the Holy Spirit. This was and still is the necessary means for salvation. Certainly, God is not bound by the sacraments, and so God who reads hearts and who understands when baptism is not a possibility can also bring an individual to salvation in His own way. Nevertheless, the waters of baptism are the ordinary way in which the possibility for the gift of salvation begins.

A part of my morning ritual is to take a shower. Standing under the spray of water, I am reminded that I am baptized into Jesus' life. I am baptized to live my life once again today as a member of Christ's Mystical Body. I am to "put on Christ" and to recognize the opportunities that will come my way. As I stand under the cleansing shower, I am also reminded of some physical scars on my chest as a result of past surgeries. For me, those scars represent wounds I have endured in my body. Then I am reminded that in my Christian life I also have wounds which are caused by my own sinful actions where I have chosen evil over good. With regard to the physical scars I bear, surgery took away the duodenal ulcer, the gallstones and the gall bladder, but the scars remain. Christ's surgical procedure on my behalf, His act of complete self-surrender to the Father's will as He hung upon the cross, has taken away my sins and the sins of the world. Christ's surgery removes the scars and He replaces sin with the ointment leading to salvation. We have been baptized, immersed into God's love in a way that will endure forever just as Jesus promised He will be with us forever.

Each day I have opportunities to say *"Serviam"* or *"Non serviam."* Standing daily in the shower is a brief reminder that I will have those opportunities during this day. The morning ritual of showering allows me to remember I have the chance to serve God, the chance to renounce evil, and the blessing of asking the Holy Spirit to deepen His gifts within me.

From the Catechism of the Catholic Church:
The Catechism of the Catholic Church highlights the coming of the Holy Spirit and the words of promise Jesus spoke to His disciples. It also reminds us that it is the Holy Spirit who forms the Church in the life of prayer.

> On the day of Pentecost, the Spirit of the Promise was poured out on the disciples, gathered "together in one place." While awaiting the Spirit, "all these with one accord devoted themselves to prayer." The Spirit who teaches the Church and recalls for her everything that Jesus said was also to form her in the life of prayer.[23]

The Catechism also reminds us that when we pray to Christ, it is the grace of the Holy Spirit working within us which prompts our desire to pray. Yearning for the fire of the Holy Spirit is implicitly stated in the following paragraph from the Catechism:

> "No one can say 'Jesus is Lord' except by the Holy Spirit." Every time we begin to pray to Jesus it is the Holy Spirit who draws us on the way of prayer by his prevenient grace. Since he teaches us to pray by recalling Christ, how could we not pray to the Spirit too? That is why the Church invites us to call upon the Holy Spirit every day, especially at the beginning and the end of every important action.[24]

---

23 Catechism of the Catholic Church, para. 2623.
24 *Ibid.*, para. 2670.

Reflection questions:

- Do I *really* believe that the Holy Spirit dwells within me as a result of my baptism into Christ? If so, what difference has this made in my life?
- How deeply do I desire the fire of the Holy Spirit in my life?
- Does thinking about the Holy Spirit as the *promise* of Jesus do anything to help shape my understanding of who the Holy Spirit is?
- Which gift of the Holy Spirit (wisdom, understanding, right judgment, knowledge, courage, reverence, wonder and awe in the presence of God) do I desire most at this point in my life?
- Who are some of the people who have shown me what it is like to have the fire of the Holy Spirit within them?

> *A clean heart create for me, God;*
> *renew in me a steadfast spirit.*
> *Do not drive me from your presence,*
> *nor take away from me your holy spirit.*
> *Restore my joy in your salvation;*
> *sustain in me a willing spirit.*
> Ps 51:12-14

Chapter 5

Exposing Myself to the One Who Knows Me Well

Scripture's insight:

It is embarrassing enough for the self-conscious person who may have a speech impediment or a limp in his or her walk, but imagine the embarrassment resulting from noticeable blood stains due to hemorrhage. Imagine also the embarrassment felt by a reticent individual who prefers to remain unnoticed when suddenly catapulted into notoriety.

The woman mentioned in Mark 5:25-34 could easily have felt both those types of embarrassment. For twelve years she had been afflicted with a hemorrhage problem, most likely a problem with steady menstrual bleeding. According to Old Testament ritual laws, she would have been considered "unclean," thereby adding a social stigma to the physical problem she endured. Added to this problem, the woman had been trying to find doctors to help her for those twelve years and had exhausted her finances.

One could easily understand how a woman who had this condition would be very self-conscious. Walking around with a social stigma is enough to lower self-esteem; the physical problem only worsened, and the money was gone. Pretty embarrassing. But then she heard Jesus was close by. She knew that others had been cured by Him. In her unassuming but carefully-planned attempt, she approached Him as He walked by and simply touched the garment that He was wearing. Wonder of wonders, she felt an immediate healing. The blood flow dried up.

Just as immediately, however, Jesus stopped, turned toward the crowd following Him, and said, "Who has touched my clothes?" His disciples wanted to keep moving since they were heading toward the home of a synagogue official whose daughter was ill. The disciples tried to reason with Jesus, suggesting that with such a large crowd following Him, it was inevitable that someone would bump up against Him. Jesus was undeterred; He kept looking around to see who had touched His garment.

What must have been running through the woman's mind at that particular moment? She probably could have died a thousand deaths, realizing that Jesus wanted her to acknowledge what she had done. If she remained silent, would He dismiss the incident? She was the woman who had been "unclean," and making herself known in this large setting of people was something she feared. How would they react? How would Jesus respond? Did she regret having come out on that day to see Jesus and touch Him?

She approached Jesus in fear and trembling. The shaking of her body and the look on her face must have told Jesus exactly what she was feeling. Then she knelt down before Jesus and told Him the whole story. Was she looking into His eyes as she told Him what had happened? I don't know for sure, but I assume so. She exposed the disconcerting situation of her health in a moment which was truly embarrassing while many eyes would have been focused on her.

Jesus saw the transparency of her life in those few moments. He had to know how difficult this was for her. He appreciated her faith in Him and spoke with the most assuring and tender voice, "Go in peace." I wonder how long He continued to watch her, perhaps glancing back occasionally as He continued on to Jairus' home. I also wonder how long the smile remained on her face, knowing that she was cured, that the social stigma was removed, and that her life was made whole. One brief encounter is all it took; the gift of peace Jesus wished for her would be the long-lasting result. The peace she felt also resulted in physical healing and in her newly found self-worth.

The insight of companions who experience the waters:
When we hear about someone "exposing" himself or herself, we frequently associate this behavior with perversion. Obviously, this is not what is referred to here. Rather, in the context of prayer, exposing oneself deals not with perversion but with *con*-version.

Much is written today about the "theology of the body," utilizing the material given by Pope John Paul II in the first five years of his pontificate during his Wednesday general audiences. In the most sacred of contexts, the body is truly the hallmark of God's creation. When we consider what a marvel the body is, we can see all the more clearly the types of perversions which exist with the debasement and degradation of the body.

Again, quoting from Mother Mary Francis, P.C.C., whose own body experienced the moment of death in February of 2006, we have several beautiful insights about the body:

> Our bodies are so noble. The infamous carnal sinners of history are, not those who loved their bodies too much, but those who loved their bodies too little. They are those who failed to respect or perhaps even to understand the dignity of that masterpiece of the Father, the human body. It is a creation so marvelous that the Father did not hesitate to give it to his own divine, eternal, infinite, all-comprehensive expression of himself in the Incarnation of the Son, in the same way that it is given to us and with the same senses and faculties possessed by our own bodies.[25]

Mother Mary Francis reminds us that the greatest sinners failed to respect their bodies – they loved their bodies too little. When one loves his or her body too little, the result is often doing things which dishonor the nobility of the body. Some who love their bodies too little perform acts of self-mutilation; others perform acts whereby the body functions at a debased level, allowing their bodies to be tools of gratification rather than the finely-tuned instruments which are made in the image and likeness of God.

The woman with the hemorrhage (Mk 5:25-34) respected her body. Although plagued with a physical and social cross, she respected herself enough to want to be made whole. For this to happen in its fullness she needed to expose herself to Jesus who wanted to know who had touched His clothing. In that self-exposing moment, bringing before Jesus the embarrassment and humiliation of

---

[25] Mother Mary Francis, P.C.C., *Anima Christi: Soul of Christ* (San Francisco: Ignatius Press, 2001) 22.

her life, she found the One who knew her and loved her so intimately. The priest psychologist and spiritual anchor for many, Fr. Benedict J. Groeschel, writes tongue-in-cheek:

> Faced with the awful reality of sin, many of us feel rotten about ourselves. We see our own weaknesses, our own failings, our own frightening temptations, and we become very disappointed. As a priest, I have heard the confessions of many people: ordinary and famous, peddlers and prelates, even some saintly people. I have discovered that we are *all* disappointed in ourselves – everyone, that is, except those who suffer from paranoia. That's how you can tell they're crazy! They're not disappointed in *themselves* – just in everybody else.[26]

When one exposes himself or herself before God, standing naked, as it were, and bringing to God the weaknesses, failings, temptations, sins and disappointments, it can become a moment of grace. Isn't that what the sacrament of reconciliation is all about – a moment of grace? Isn't that what true forgiveness between friends is all about – a moment of grace? Exposing ourselves to the One who knows us so well, who knows the physical hemorrhage as well as the social stigma, who knows the reticence as well as the desire to be healed, is truly a moment of grace.

I will quote once again from Fr. Groeschel:

> St. John of the Cross said, "I saw that there was a river that every soul must cross who would come to the kingdom of heaven. The name of that river is sorrow and the boat on which we cross it is called love." And love does not permit us to fail. Why do we forget time and again that God loves us?[27]

It was Saint Augustine who reminded early Christians that even in their darkest nights, God was listening. The same God works in the same way today. When we come to God in our darkest nights, we are exposing our darkness to the radiance of God's light. What better consolation can there be? The Easter proclamation reminds

---

26 Fr. Benedict J. Groeschel, C.F.R., *Healing the Original Wound: Reflections on the Full Meaning of Salvation* (Cincinnati, Ohio: Servant Books, 1993) 27.
27 *Ibid.*, 40.

us that the light dispels darkness. We are called to be saints, to grow in holiness. A saint first recognizes that he is a sinner. A saint first recognizes the need for restoration, which comes from God alone. A saint is one who believes in the message of the Easter proclamation – Christ indeed does dispel the darkness of sin. The crucial point is getting enough courage to touch the clothing of Jesus and then to acknowledge that it was I who touched His garment.

How exposing myself to the One who knows me well can be nurtured:

Jesus said to the woman who touched His clothing, "Go in peace." For a long time now I have tried to practice a modified version of the *Examen* which Saint Ignatius of Loyola asked of his confreres. It is a method of self-examination which looks at one's daily activity. Are there areas where sin occurred? Are there areas where Christ-like love could have been better shown? Are there opportunities where integrity of heart can be experienced?

To practice this version of the *Examen*, I use a five-point method of reflection. This is something I choose to do every night before I go to bed. To some degree, it allows me to expose myself to the One who knows me well. Also, and I believe this is very important, it allows me to hear Jesus say, "Go in peace." The five points draw from the acronym "peace."

1. **PRESENCE**: I place myself in the presence of God, finding a suitable place for prayer and reflection. In the presence of God, I allow myself the necessary time to slow down, to realize that the moment spent in God's presence is a blessed opportunity, and I simply remember that God's presence is one of love.

2. **EXPERIENCES**: I bring to prayer the experiences of my day. Often the experiences are the moments of interaction with other individuals. This provides me with ample opportunity to see how I acted: Did I respond with kindness, mercy, compassion? Was I rude, perfunctory, annoyed? Other experiences upon which I reflect are my own sins of

commission and *omission*. As I reflect upon the experiences of each day, I see many areas where I need God's grace to grow in holiness. I also uncover movements of growth which may be occurring, thanks be to God. It is the recognition of these experiences which helps me to expose my true identity to God.

3. **ACTIVITY:** In this part of the prayer, I focus on God's divine activity. I realize it is God's initiative which draws me to come to Him. I also realize that God's activity, God's breath, God's Holy Spirit can and do transform the experiences of my own life. It was God's activity in the power of Christ which gave healing to the hemorrhaging woman. It is also God's activity in the power of Christ and through the Holy Spirit which brings light to dispel the darkness within me.

4. **COMMITMENT:** In order for this process to be fruitful I think about an area in which I can live better the Christian life to which I am called. I look at the events and experiences of that particular day, and I try to find one area on which I can focus my efforts toward improvement or rehabilitation.

5. **ENLIGHTENMENT:** The *Examen* prayer begins by recognizing the presence of God in my life; it concludes by recognizing that I need God's ongoing presence to enlighten me. I will be conscious of the commitment I have made for the next day, but I ask God to enlighten me to see when the opportunity might arise. In this prayer, I ask for the ability to recognize the movement of God's grace.

When we come before the Lord in prayer, exposing the limitations and the positive movements occurring within us, we need to know that God hears us.

This brings me to a very serious issue voiced by many: What about the times when prayer seems not to be answered? C. S. Lewis is said to have commented that when we meet the Lord in heaven, we will be so grateful to Him for the times He did not answer our prayers the way we had wanted. This thought may offer consolation as we review the times when certain prayers were not answered as we wanted, but still we are left with the question of why prayer sometimes seems not to be answered. Some of the more common answers range from suggesting that we may be unworthy to receive the request we made in prayer, all the way to God's knowing better what we truly need.

Another question regarding prayer is to ask how prayer *is* answered. There are two main ways to look at the question. One follows an approach in which God, beyond the confines of this world, hears and responds in those moments when we unite with Him in prayer. The other approach is one of flesh and blood, where God is in the world and working through women and men of good will. This is a specifically Christian approach whereby, because of Jesus' Incarnation into human history and His continued presence in His followers, we are able to be the Body of Christ for others.

Perhaps an example will help. In a "God beyond the world" approach to prayer, I pray to God and desire that God will intervene and actually do the work to set up all the conditions so my prayer can be answered. I pray, for example, for a parishioner who is experiencing depression. I ask God to help her, to lift her spirits. This approach allows me to pray and bring my good petition to God. It stops there, a prayer between God and me, and I wait for God to do whatever is necessary to lift my parishioner's depression. Days later I find that she has been hospitalized and her depression has grown in severity. My conclusion with this approach: God did not answer my prayer. When I ask why not, answers I give to myself can lead me to grow more skeptical of Jesus' words about asking and receiving. Then why didn't I receive? Why would I want to expose myself to a non-responsive God? We're back to the question of why certain prayers seem not to be answered. How come?

The other approach, "God in the world," is an approach which involves human beings in their bodies doing in their bodies what Christ would do. Christ, in other words, continues to exist within us. Our hands and feet continue the work of Christ. Thus, we become an extension of the love of Christ. Although the human body of *Jesus* returned to heaven long ago, the Body of *Christ* remains with us. We can extend the work of Christ who is present with us because we are part of Christ's body. Using the example above, the "God in the world" approach to prayer means I will not only pray and ask God to bring healing to the depressed woman; I will send a card, make a phone call, visit, bring a gift. This approach involves some activity on my part. When I bring this request to prayer, I am asking God to help me discern what is the best thing I can do as a member of Christ's Mystical Body with regard to the intention for which I pray.

Both approaches are good and beneficial. With either approach, I need to trust that God's Holy Spirit is active. In the "God beyond the world" approach, I need to believe that the Holy Spirit does hear my request, and that God through His Spirit will bring about what is right so His ultimate plan can be fulfilled and He can best be glorified. With the second approach, I need to believe that the Holy Spirit is the energy allowing me to discover what I need to do and what part I can play to bring about the request I have made of God.

A final thought: when I was a little boy my father would on occasion let me put my hands on the steering wheel of the car and even do some of the steering while he remained in control of the vehicle. By analogy, the "God beyond the world" approach leaves the driving to God and I remain a passenger; with the "God in the world" approach, God puts my hands on the steering wheel and I actually do some of the driving while the Holy Spirit remains in control.

From the Catechism of the Catholic Church:

God, in a very real manner, exposed to the world His love by giving us Jesus, the only-begotten Son. Jesus, in His human nature, was exposed to sinful situations as well as good. Jesus also exposed His own thoughts and feelings on many occasions, revealing His love for God the Father and for the Father's children. Jesus' body was exposed, like all of our own, at the moment of birth. His body was also exposed for all to see as He hung upon the cross, nearly naked and bloodied. All of these experiences which the Son of God encountered and endured were accepted because of love.

The Catechism reminds us of this love relationship God has with us:

> God calls man first. Man may forget his Creator or hide far from his face; he may run after idols or accuse the deity of having abandoned him; yet the living and true God tirelessly calls each person to that mysterious encounter known as prayer. In prayer, the faithful God's initiative of love always comes first; our own first step is always a response. As God gradually reveals himself and reveals man to himself, prayer appears as a reciprocal call, a covenant drama. Through words and actions, this drama engages the heart. It unfolds throughout the whole history of salvation.[28]

Reflection questions:
- What obstacles do I need to overcome in order to bring myself to touch the garment of Jesus?
- Have I any experiences in my life where I felt touched by the healing power of Jesus?
- We all have secrets we try to keep from others; what secret, if I were to tell it to the Lord, would most expose me as I truly am?
- Can I hear Jesus telling me to go in peace?

> *You formed my inmost being;*
> *you knit me in my mother's womb.*
> *I praise you, so wonderfully you made me;*
> *Wonderful are your works!*
> *My very self you knew.*
>   Ps 139:13-1

---

28 Catechism of the Catholic Church, para. 2567.

Chapter 6

Resting in Love

Scripture's insight:

When I think of the theme of "resting in love," three images from Scripture come to mind. First, I imagine the Infant Jesus being held so closely in the arms of Mary and Joseph. Scenes of the Nativity usually portray Jesus in the manger while Mary, Joseph, and perhaps shepherds surround Him. But when we allow our imagination to reveal the more complete picture, we can see the Infant being held tenderly by His mother and foster father. We can imagine Mary fondling the Infant, caressing Him with tender care, and attending to His every physical need. Also, if we allow our imagination to think about the time when Jesus was nurtured in Mary's womb, we can appreciate how His Heart lay right underneath her own. The Holy Child was resting in the love of His mother; the tender mother must also have been resting, contemplating how it was that she had been chosen to hold this gift of love for all humankind. It was a reciprocal moment of rest.

Secondly, I am drawn into the moment when Simeon (Lk 2:25-35) took the child in his arms and proclaimed, "Now, Master, you may let your servant go in peace ... for my eyes have seen your salvation." Certainly, it was the Baby Jesus who rested in the loving arms of Simeon, a person whom the Gospel tells us was righteous and devout. Jesus rested in the loving arms of Simeon; Simeon, likewise, was able to rest in the loving arms of God, and in this instant he also realized that he held the loving God in his own arms. It was a reciprocal moment of rest.

Thirdly, in the moments before Jesus' crucifixion and death, while at supper with His disciples, Jesus was troubled. He had just washed the feet of His disciples (Jn 13:1-20) and then said, "Amen, amen, I say to you, one of you will betray me" (13:21). The disciples who were gathered with Him looked at each other and wondered what these words meant. The beloved disciple, "the one whom Jesus loved" (13:23), was seated next to Jesus. He leaned back against Jesus' chest, asking who it could be. This encounter between Jesus and John, and in a certain sense among Jesus and the other disciples, is an encounter of love. John, leaning against the chest of Jesus, was literally resting in love. Jesus, troubled and with terrible anguish, was also able in that brief moment to rest in the love of John and the other disciples. It was a reciprocal moment of rest.

In prayer, we are able to rest in the love of God, the love of Jesus. Have we ever given thought to the possibility that Jesus might also be resting in the love we have for Him? Could our time spent in prayer possibly be a reciprocal moment of rest?

The insight of companions who experience the waters:
St. Francis de Sales (1567-1622), bishop of Geneva, Switzerland, wrote in his classic book, *Introduction to the Devout Life*, that any of us in the most ordinary of circumstances can live saintly lives. He encouraged spiritual practices, chief among them the practice of prayer. Later in his life he met Jane Frances de Chantal, a widow who eventually consecrated her life to God. With her he founded the Order of the Visitation Sisters in 1610. Her brother also became a bishop, and to him Francis de Sales wrote: "Say little and say it well, and it amounts to a great deal." When one rests in the love of Christ, one does not have to say much at all. Prayer is essentially a response to God's gracious and mighty deeds of salvation. Faced with that overwhelming mystery, sometimes the greatest response we can give is simply to remain in awed love.

St. Alphonsus Ligouri (1696-1787) penned a prayer which insightfully reminds us how we can rest in the love of Christ. His prayer is called the "Prayer Before Sleep."

> Jesus Christ, my God,
> I adore you and thank you for all the graces
> you have given me this day.
> I offer you my sleep and all the moments of this night,
> and I ask you to keep me from sin.

> I put myself within your sacred side and
> under the mantle of our Lady.
> Let your holy angels stand about me and keep me in peace.
> And let your blessing be upon me. Amen.

This prayer expresses, at least implicitly, a belief in God Who does not turn His eyes away from us. Resting in His love allows us to turn our eyes toward Him. Resting in love allows us to be amazed by Him, amazed by His constancy and care. St. Bernard of Clairvaux (c.1090-1153) wrote: "See with what mutual embraces of affection you must love and embrace him in return, he who has valued you at such a great price."[29] When that occurs, we are resting in His love.

Years ago, while I was attending a Catholic university, an instructor told me the administration and faculty want students to succeed. Therefore, the university treats students as though a protective net were underneath, keeping them from falling into failure. The student who works hard and remains diligent will have the protective net under him or her. Rainer Maria Rilke speaks about a similar protective hand of God who embraces us and allows us to rest in Him:

> We all are falling. This hand falls.
> And look at others: it is in them all.
> And yet there is one who holds this falling
> Endlessly gently in His hands.[30]

How resting in love can be nurtured:

When I read the lives of the saints or of other individuals who are considered to be models of holiness, I notice that they describe time spent in prayer as an opportunity to rest in God's Divine Love. I am glad these models of prayerful holiness are not all the same. Each of their personalities is quite different and they show us that not all prayer methods are the same or need to be the same. The

---

29 Sister Agnes Lemaire, *Saint Bernard et le mystère du Christ* (Quebec: Anne Sigier, 1991) 43.
30 Regis Martin, *The Last Things: Death, Judgment, Heaven, Hell* (San Francisco: Ignatius Press, 1998) 39.

diversity and variety of prayer forms found in these exemplary lives reminds me that each of us will find certain prayers (or prayer styles) to be helpful and other prayers (or prayer styles) not as helpful in our relationship with Christ.

For example, a prayer which for a long time has been a favorite of mine is the *Anima Christi*. It provides images and thoughts which lead to the experience of resting in a close relationship with Christ. This prayer, like many others, is part of the Church's treasury of prayers. One translation of the prayer is as follows:

> Soul of Christ, sanctify me.
> Body of Christ, save me.
> Blood of Christ, inebriate me.
> Water from the side of Christ, wash me.
> Passion of Christ, strengthen me.
>
> O good Jesus, hear me.
> Within your wounds, hide me.
> Separated from you let me never be.
> From the deceitful enemy, defend me.
> In the hour of my death, call me,
> And close to you, bid me come,
> That with your saints,
> I may praise you forever and ever. Amen.

Of the many prayer experiences which allow us to rest in love, the ones I am going to mention in brief fashion are these: engaging in prayer trips, making use of a word or phrase as a basis for prayer, being like John as he rested on Jesus' chest and asked a question, and to conclude, resting in the arms of our Blessed Mother.

1. Prayer journeys. Prayer trips, sometimes called prayer journeys, are opportunities to enter into contemplation which is a long, loving gaze upon God. Our breathing becomes deeper and with each breath we become more aware of the presence of God's Holy Spirit. Prayer trips are a form of guided meditation, allowing our imagination to bring us to a place where we can encounter the living Lord Jesus. In a prayer journey we go in imagination to a favorite place of ours and as we explore the surroundings, we are met by Jesus. We have a chance to hear what Jesus desires to speak to us. We have a chance to speak to Him as well, letting Jesus know exactly what is in our heart at that moment. We may walk together in silence or we may converse. We might discuss a problem, a hope, a dream, a sorrow. What is important in this type of prayer is to rest with a confidence that Jesus is with us and that His love is all we truly need.

2. A word or phrase as a springboard. A second way to rest in love is to make use of a word or phrase repeated for a period of time. One of the beautiful examples of this type of prayer is found in the Jesus Prayer (sometimes known as the Prayer of the Heart). In the anonymous Russian novel entitled *The Way of the Pilgrim,* we encounter a young man who desires to grow in prayer. In the story, the *starets* (a wisdom figure) leads the apprentice in the way of prayer by having him say over and over these words: *Lord Jesus Christ, Son of the Living God, have mercy on me, a sinner.* This form of prayer is one example of how we can become all the more conscious of the mystery of God's life in us. There are many short phrases from Scripture which also can provide beautiful springboards to prayer. Sometimes even a word itself can be of assistance in drawing us to the center – to Jesus Himself. I personally like the phrase which accompanies the portrait of Divine Mercy as given by St. Faustina: *Jesus, I trust in you.* Other times I find myself praying with Jesus' words from the cross when He said, *"I thirst."*

If these words or phrases allow us to rest in love, and indeed they can, then this form of prayer is helpful. The phrase *Jesus, I trust in you*, is beneficial under many circumstances. When burdened by temptation or by decisions we need to make, the phrase reminds us that Jesus is nearby. When we seek a particular gift and wonder whether it is right for us, the phrase reminds us that Jesus knows what is best not only for us but also for the bigger picture around us. When praying the phrase *"I thirst,"* perhaps we will hear Jesus as the one speaking those words and we may be able to provide Him with a quenching drink. If so, we are resting in love as we accompany Him in His agony. On the other hand, we may be the one who calls out those words and we can again rest in love, this time believing that Jesus is providing the drink.[31]

3. Ask Jesus questions. Thirdly, as John reclined next to the Lord during the Last Supper, he rested his head on Jesus' chest and asked the question, "Who is it, Lord?" Resting in Jesus' love for us allows us to ask questions. He welcomes them; He also allows us to hear the beating of His heart if we are resting closely and with the silence to hear.

Of course, when we ask questions, we usually make petitions – things for ourselves or intercessions for others. We also know Jesus does not always give what we ask for; what He does give to us, a gift more precious than all else, is the gift of Himself. "Ask," Jesus says, "and you shall receive." Even when we do not receive specifically what we ask for, nevertheless, we do receive. We receive the gift of Jesus' presence. He cannot do otherwise. It is the nature of Jesus to give, to love, to allow us to find rest in Him. In Jesus' own words He tells us, "Come to me, all you who labor and are burdened, and I will give you rest ... you will find rest for yourselves. For my yoke is easy and my burden light" (Mt 11-28-30).

4. Prayer to Mary. To conclude this section I would like to mention occasions of prayer to Mary. If ever we associate the image of resting in love, we can think of the many opportunities Jesus would have had to rest in the loving presence of His mother. Can you hear her giving a word of encouragement to Jesus when He accomplished a project? Can you see her smiling at Jesus when He told her about an event in His day? Can you feel the sword that pierced her heart as she held the body of her Son when He had been taken down from the cross? She is our mother as well, in moments of joy and sorrow. To call upon her, to be in her presence, to look at her with a childlike trust, to confide in her as a son or daughter – all of this and more is what occurs when we turn our attention to her. In a profound way, it is she who gives us familiarity with the mystery we only begin to fathom in Christ.

---

31 A helpful work to further this understanding of the Jesus Prayer is entitled *The Name of Jesus* by Fr. Irenee Hausherr, S.J., (Kalamazoo, Michigan: Cistercian Publications, Inc., 1978).

From the Catechism of the Catholic Church:
In the New Covenant, prayer is the living relationship of the children of God with their Father who is good beyond measure, with his Son Jesus Christ and with the Holy Spirit. The grace of the Kingdom is "the union of the entire holy and royal Trinity ... with the whole human spirit." Thus, the life of prayer is the habit of being in the presence of the thrice-holy God and in communion with him. This communion of life is always possible because, through Baptism, we have already been united with Christ. Prayer is *Christian* insofar as it is communion with Christ and extends throughout the Church, which is his Body. Its dimensions are those of Christ's love.[32]

Reflection questions:
- Can I recall any moment when I felt like I was resting in God's love?
- Have I ever thought about Jesus resting in the love I have for Him?
- Does the idea of a word or phrase appeal to me as a way of resting in love? If so, what word or phrase might I consider using?
- What is my relationship like with Jesus' mother? Do I believe she is also my mother who loves me in a most tender way?
- What is the best aspect of being able to rest in love?

> *Lord, my heart is not proud;*
> *nor are my eyes haughty.*
> *I do not busy myself with great matters,*
> *with things too sublime for me.*
> *Rather, I have stilled my soul,*
> *hushed it like a weaned child.*
> *Like a weaned child on its mother's lap,*
> *so is my soul within me.*
> Ps 131:1-2

---

[32] Catechism of the Catholic Church, para. 2565.

Concluding Thought: Why Pray?

Why pray? Perhaps the Weekday Preface IV in the Roman Missal used in the Catholic liturgy sets a tone to answer the question: "Our prayer of thanksgiving adds nothing to your greatness, but makes us grow in your grace." Paraphrased, this prayer suggests that like many aspects of life, it is good for us. How? Prayer keeps us aware of the importance of God in our lives. If God is not important, then prayer will not matter. It would probably be a waste of time. However, if God *is* important, then prayer keeps us aware of the relationship we have with Him. Prayer helps us to remain attuned to the Paschal Mystery of Jesus Christ which also has the opportunity to unfold in our life. In other words, prayer keeps us open to the workings of God and specifically God's Holy Spirit in our lives. Prayer allows us to understand that the Paschal Mystery continues for each of us. It also allows us to be more sensitive to the needs of others. When we pray, we often think of others and some of their experiences. If prayer keeps us open, open to God and to neighbor, then prayer serves a very important purpose, for it helps us put into practice the two great commandments of Jesus: to love God with our whole heart, strength, mind and soul, and to love our neighbor as ourselves. So why pray? Succinctly, prayer provides strength, awareness, and an openness to the Paschal Mystery, and helps us to grow in hope and love.

Saint Augustine is remembered for this salient reminder: "You have made us for yourself, Lord, and our hearts are restless until they rest in You." In these pages we have examined the topic of prayer as heart-to-heart conversation with God, and we have reflected upon prayer as resting in God's love. While there are many ways to describe prayer, one essential element of every description is that *prayer is based on love of God*. We cannot pray if we do not love. The important step here is to understand what true love of God is all about. Jesus said that the first and greatest commandment was to love God. Therefore, love of God (meaning love *for* God) is foundational to prayer. Love, while associated with feelings, at a deeper and more profound level is not a feeling; love is a decision. It is a decision made by individuals and also a decision made by an apostolic community who pray to the one true God in various ways but always with a common mission to live on in Christ's love. Pope Benedict XVI explains this point so beautifully in his encyclical *Deus Caritas Est.*

In my relationship with God, I can be committed to love Him. I may not know the *why* to many things that happen; I don't need to. What I need to know is that God loves me – God loves all of humanity made in His image and likeness. God, in His love for us, continues to make decisions in our best interest. This is the measure of true love – wanting what is best for the other. My love for God, therefore, is a decision about wanting what is best for the building of God's Kingdom and wanting what is best so that the message of Christ, truly God, can be furthered.

Saint Paul's letter to the Corinthians provides an excellent tool for examination to help us determine whether our love for God and love for others is real. He writes: "Love is patient, love is kind. It is not jealous, is not pompous, it is not inflated, it is not rude, it does not seek its own interests, it is not quick-tempered, it does not brood over injury, it does not rejoice over wrongdoing but rejoices with the truth. It bears all things, believes all things, hopes all things, endures all things. Love never fails" (1 Cor 13:4-8).

If prayer is based on love, then we know that as love manifests itself in many and various ways, so too does prayer. In these pages the image of water has been used to describe the life of prayer. The Catechism of the Catholic Church reminds us: "The Holy Spirit is the *living water* 'welling up to eternal life' in the heart that prays. It is he who teaches us to accept it at its source: Christ."[33]

Since the Holy Spirit is the water "welling up to eternal life," we are reminded that it is our response in love, our prayer, and our life in the Holy Spirit which are destined toward eternal life.

---

33 *Ibid.*, para. 2652.

Who are the ones most often in the water? More often than not, we would say it is the young. However, chronological age really has little to do with who enters the water since young people well into their eighties or nineties also spend considerable time in the pool. Youthfulness is all about remaining close to the source of life. A young child, for example, is relatively close to the beginning of his or her human life. By analogy, prayer helps us to remain youthful, for it is the perfect means to keep us close to the Source of life. Perhaps Jesus had this thought in mind when He said, "Unless you turn and become like children, you will not enter the kingdom of heaven" (Mt 18:3).

The Letter to the Hebrews (13:14) reminds us that "here we have no lasting city." In Job 19:25-26 we read: "I know that my Redeemer lives … whom I myself shall see: my own eyes, not another's, shall behold him, and from my flesh I shall see God." As we grow older and realize the vulnerability of human life, we become more acutely aware that "here we have no lasting city." Our lives are destined for something further; we are made in God's image and likeness and in time, we shall behold Him face to face. Prayer, step by step during our earthly sojourn, readies us for the overwhelming meeting which shall take place when our days here have ended. I would be filled with delight when the time comes for my personal meeting with the Lord, if He were to say, "Thank you for the times you spoke with me and listened to me in prayer; I've been waiting to welcome you home. Come on in and be immersed in the waters of life."